D1622329

The
She
Book v.2

Tanya Markul

Andrews McMeel
PUBLISHING®

Other books by Tanya Markul
The She Book

Andrews McMeel Publishing
a division of Andrews McMeel Universal
1130 Walnut Street, Kansas City, Missouri 64106

www.andrewsmcmeel.com

20 21 22 23 24 BVG 10 9 8 7 6 5 4 3 2 1

ISBN: 978-1-5248-6081-3

Library of Congress Control Number: 2018966057

Editor: Katie Gould
Designer: Diane Marsh
Production Editor: Amy Strassner
Production Manager: Carol Coe
Illustration by Tim Bjørn

ATTENTION: SCHOOLS AND BUSINESSES
Andrews McMeel books are available at quantity discounts with bulk purchase for educational, business, or sales promotional use. For information, please e-mail the Andrews McMeel Publishing Special Sales Department: specialsales@amuniversal.com.

to mother darkness

In darkness you're formed
and in darkness you're reborn.

This book is dedicated to everyone who unconditionally supported and encouraged me to write during my darkest hour, especially you, my beloved Christian Ryd.

how to use the book

The She Book v.2 is a continuation
of *The She Book*, starting with
passage one hundred fifteen.

There is no single or correct way to
use *The She Book* or *The She Book v.2*.

Readers call them loyal travelers and sources
of inspiration, conversation, and connection.

Use them intuitively and spontaneously. They
represent a safe and nonjudgmental space.

Tips: Weave the books into your daily rituals.
Choose a passage and make it a journaling
prompt. Share your favorite at the start of class
or use a poem to close a circle or gathering.

Let the book be what you need it to be—
words you can't find, a conversation you
wish to have, a blessing, and a gentle,
courageous companion through darkness.

To the discovery
of the wisdom
of your shadow self.

And so it is.

about the book

An intimate collection of modern prose, poems, and quotes about surviving dark times. It's about telling your story.

A resilient journey through a season of loneliness, a cycle of heartache, and a year of depression—this is what she unexpectedly found within the depths of her brokenness and how she emerged stronger.

This book unapologetically explores the feeling, healing, and revealing of depression and the power of asking for help and being open to receiving support from nature and others, while giving a creative and empowering voice to emotional pain.

This is the second book in The She Book series.

Now gather the candles and sage
and trust that when the dark part is over,
you'll be reborn come spring.

introduction

She wanted power. But what she needed was wisdom. And she'd find it in the realm of the underworld, in the belly of the great below.

These pages describe how she survived the furthest depths of her personal darkness. If you're there and ready to come up for air, she hopes these words can be the hands that guide you back to the surface.

a call to four corners

To the direction of North
To the element of Earth
May you be guided toward truth.

To the direction of East
To the element of Air
May you discover your wings.

To the direction of South
To the element of Fire
May you rise and fall like dusk and dawn.

And, to the direction of West
To the element of Water
May you always find your way.

Woman, be like water
And find your way home.

one hundred fifteen

Love, be patient with me
as I shed this skin
as I lay old patterns at God's feet
as I burn and dream
as I'm carried by this stream.
I can be fierce
while feeling this vulnerable.
I can seem far away
as my wounds drip
as I writher, cry, and hiss
as I take in this last breath.
Generous was this passing death.
Praise be the person I was
as I gasp life into
the warrior
I now am.

one hundred sixteen

When she realized that loss, abandonment, rejection, and betrayal were guiding her home, she stopped trying to rewrite the chapters of pain and allowed a story of empowerment to begin.

one hundred seventeen

What I've been afraid to say about me:

We used food stamps and ate government cheese and bread. I lived a life of hand-me-downs and borrowing from friends.

As a kid, I was forced to go to catechism. I used to lie in confession, about my dad's whereabouts, and my mom's profession.

Because I didn't know.

In first grade, I was bullied because I wore the same clothes every day. Later, I got into college, by God's good grace.

I then owed the government thirty thousand in loans. I've failed classes, driven drunk, shoplifted food and clothes.

My last family member died of a drug overdose.

I've lied about my experiences with sex. My father used to pass out drunk at the end of my bed.

I lost my best friend to a cocaine addiction. I have aunties and uncles battling alcoholism.

Their children are now in and out of prison.

During high school, I can't remember my ma not being high. I've spent summers in bars since I was five.

I had to grow up fast. I've been sexually assaulted and harassed.

Both my legal guardians died by the time I was thirteen. In my twenties, I was stoned for four years consecutively.

My grandmother had Native American blood coursing through her veins. I used to starve myself on even-numbered days.

Right now, I have cousins fighting losing battles with heroin. I used to define myself by all that is narrowing.

But as heartache can clear the slate for a new direction, I went from asking, "How sharp are the knives?" to "From my story, I need no protection."

one hundred eighteen

When I lose grace,
I remember the rain
and how she falls
with faith every time.

one hundred nineteen

Do not believe
the things
you tell yourself
while possessed
by the demons
of your inner shit.

one hundred twenty

What you couldn't see coming.
What you didn't expect.
What you weren't prepared for.
The blind side.
The black smoke.
The descent.
It will gulp your tears,
drain your blood,
and wipe your slate clean.
Game over.
That's when you bite back,
tear your gaping heart open wider,
and start again.

You start again.

one hundred twenty-one

Woman,
you can act hard,
but you're stronger
when you're soft.

one hundred twenty-two

The moment you become aware that the only thing holding you back is a disbelief in your power, or a lack of self-worth, or the voice of "You are not good enough," you kick your inner demon's ass and change everything forever and ever, and never again will be who you were.

one hundred twenty-three

You are not
the rejected one.
You are the one
who broke free.

one hundred twenty-four

What's inside of me isn't pretty, easy, or
comfortable. What's inside of me is sometimes
lonely, desperate, lost, and ordinary.
I cry.
Often.
I think of death.
A lot.
I'm not afraid to lean into suffering
or wander into aching places.
I, too, want to check out.
But I can't.
I smell fear and feel the sun setting.
I am not innocent.
And can no longer afford cheap happiness.
I'm paying attention, and you should too.
And with waves ever crashing into my
foundation, I remain here, a waking
watchtower.

I am the dark moon rising.

one hundred twenty-five

Don't tell me you don't have what it takes. Because I'm going to call bullshit 24-7. Your life isn't just about surviving. It's about thriving. And you get to choose how you take action. Because it's on you. It's all on you. Your time is now. Not tomorrow. Not when you feel good enough. It's now. And deep down, you want this for yourself. You want to know the fighter within, the one who rises above self-limiting beliefs and mediocrity. Look, nobody is going to care more about your purpose than you, but at the same time, the world's begging you to do it. Don't give up. Don't encourage self-sabotage by surrounding yourself with assholes or by catering to negativity. Sit in the darkness until it shows you a stronger you and a better way through. Be the person you met the first time you woke up to your mission. Remember her. The warrior women that came before you are proof that you can get somewhere. The story of pain that gives you every reason not to is also your source of empowerment. It is your elixir. Drink up and pass it around. Because in this fallen world, it is up to you, sister, to raise it up.

one hundred twenty-six

Draw a circle around you, woman.
Even the ocean has boundaries.

one hundred twenty-seven

No, love, no.
The world doesn't need your spiritual bypassing
or forced forgiveness.
It needs you to be brave.
And tell your story.

one hundred twenty-eight

She's the wolf you've been waiting for.
She's the bitch you love to hate.
She's the sharp side of beautiful.
She's the ecstasy of ache.
She's the angel with fire in her eyes.
She's the protective circle cast by wild
midwives.
She's not what was and what will be.
She's now.
She's presence.
She's taking responsibility.
She's a storyteller of scars.
She's a galaxy giving birth to stars.
She's undocumented and every color.
She's your grandmother, your auntie, your
sister, and your mother.
She's a protector of the innocent.
She's fierce and vigilant.
She's shouting what some ears refuse to hear,
that the shift is upon us and change is near.
She's an unselfish foundation.
She's the waking of a love nation.
She's a woman with intent to survive.
She's reminding us that we're still alive.
She's got the cure for our restless anxiety and
collective broken heart.

She's whispering in your ear, "Wake up and do your part."

one hundred twenty-nine

The scarier something is,
the bigger the chance
a part of you might die while doing it.
That part of you longs to be let go of
so a new part of you can be born.

one hundred thirty

I'm not a receptacle for your pain.

I'm not a punching bag for your fear,
a trash bag for your tears,
or a pillow for your rage.

I'm not the ground beneath your soapbox
or the air of your rant.

I'm not a porter for your baggage labeled
"I can't."

I'm not a dartboard for your triggers, your
rampage, or blame.

And I hate seeing you this way.

But, baby, I'm not a receptacle for your pain.

one hundred thirty-one

You're not a stupid girl;
stop placing your pain
next to the seashells
on your altar. And drown it
in a bathtub of lavender.
You can't complain
about a single thing.
You've got four walls,
a lover, and a hot cup of tea.
Yet today the void
feels as big as the sky.
Pain, a puppy that won't
leave your side.
But, girl, it's going to be okay.
You know your heart's
stronger than any gray day.

one hundred thirty-two

What you were born into isn't always
who you are meant to become.

one hundred thirty-three

Try, as best you can,
to channel your sadness.
Let it arrive with color
a sun-stained sky
or flowers that won't die.
Let its canvas feel kind.
And like a new beginning.

one hundred thirty-four

When people stop showing up,
they become
gorgeous milestones
along the river
of your Life.
Without hesitation,
disappointment,
or blame,
keep flowing
your way
to source.

one hundred thirty-five

I want your flames.
I want your mess.
I want your jagged little edges,
imperfection, and stress.

Don't get up.
Stay on your precious knees.
Show me who you are
without aiming to please.

I want your anger,
not your blame.
I want what's real,
what you're afraid to name.

I want your vulnerability and fire.
I want the captive secrets from your inner liar.

I want the nonfiction, not the bullshit. Masks
on the floor, I want what's moonlit.

I'll show you mine, if you show me yours.
Without shame, we can take responsibility for
love's new course.
Now.

one hundred thirty-six

Let yourself
be unrecognizable.
Sink into your silence,
solitude, and contemplation.
No one can truly understand
what it's like to be you.
Only you.
So, pursue your truth,
and the world will
open its
curtains before you.

one hundred thirty-seven

The men in my life haven't always been this loving, sensitive, empathetic, creative, honest, or real. But I know that the wounds of my blood stop with me and won't be passed on to my sons.

I will carry these arrows close, nestle them in my quiver, and tend to them until my last breath.

"Sleep, my arrows. Sleep."

When it's my time, I will ask they be reborn as two rainbows, a field of bright red poppies, or a handsome forest lined with pines.

I won't let the poison be passed on as anything other than beauty and life. I suppose that's what a giant salty ocean between you and your inevitably decaying roots can do. I suppose that's what a prayer and a wish for love can do.

~To Ending the Legacy of Pain

one hundred thirty-eight

I asked,
How can I midwife this sadness?
How do I create a life with it?
And the night answered:
Tell your story.
Plant flowers.
That's it.

one hundred thirty-nine

I sat in the arms of sadness.
  She said she couldn't stay.

I held hands with happiness.
She said she'd soon go away.

I let myself be carried by love.
She said she'd hold me forever.

one hundred forty

Because you're stronger than you think.

And better than you feel.

~Note to Self

one hundred forty-one

I'm more than I used to be and less of what I
imagined I always was. I'm finished, yet starting
again. I'm almost off and nearly on. I'm a
pillow and blades. I'm horned and haloed.
I'm a child in a woman's body and a woman
learning to nurture her inner girl. I feel who
I am, yet know not the one I'll become. I'm
blessed and burdened, less and more, river and
desert, soft like feathers and sharp as knives.

one hundred forty-two

Hey, mermaid,
Life is either
a waterdrop
or an ocean
depending on
the depth of
your courage.

one hundred forty-three

Thank you, generous one,
for allowing me to sit at your table,
to sip your generosity, and nibble
on your wisdom.

Thank you for encouraging
me to live free. Thank you
for your grace and loving care.

To every curve, shape, and gesture
of your love, to the way you ease
my mind, I thank God you're a giver.

Thank God,
you're a giver.

'Cause the world
is hungry
for all
you've got.

one hundred forty-four

When a woman speaks from her heart, when she tells her story of pain, she may not get a response. Some might look away. Some might pretend not to hear. She could be labeled crazy. She could be considered out of control. But all it takes is one person feeling the humanity in her heart to make a revolution happen. That is how change is born. And how we begin to give a voice to the voiceless and to all those suffering who can't make it out alone—who won't survive without our stories.

one hundred forty-five

Love doesn't die.
Love doesn't get lost in the dark.
Yet I'm afraid
to let it hold me
during the hardest parts.

one hundred forty-six

When in darkness
that feels lonely
and intense
and your words
do nothing
for describing
how you feel
paint your emotions
take them for a walk
dip them in chocolate
then describe them
in one thousand surprising metaphors.

one hundred forty-seven

We
are
reborn
from
the
weight
of
our
scars.

Remember,
unbearable
pressure
gives
birth
to stars.

one hundred forty-eight

Friend, I wish you would have sought
shelter in my heart instead of building
those walls around you.

Because you showed me a country
of life and how to light up the night.
You said, "Give me your hand."
And I laughed, "Keep going!"

Back then your pain was hard to
notice behind the
bottles and smiles.

But when your loneliness started to feel
like eternity and the drugs
stole your laughter, I knew
the decade of us had fallen
off your altar.

Love, I can't help but to still
have faith
in your magic.

one hundred forty-nine

Your soul knows
what your heart
doesn't just yet.

(That you can heal.)

one hundred fifty

I wanted to give my pain
a new place to live.
So I put it onto pages
and we both moved on.
One became a story.
The other a survivor.

one hundred fifty-one

Time and again, I have known the landscape
of unhappiness and the companion of the
moon. I've survived every dark night.
So why do I still fear what I can become?

one hundred fifty-two

The peeling of the onion
the blossoming of the flower
the removal of the veils
the changing of night and day
the feeling
the healing
and the revealing
of you
is telling your story.

one hundred fifty-three

You knew what you were getting into.
Not a wading pool.
No shallow water.
But the depth of open ocean.

Not a candle.
No flickering flame.
But a raging forest fire.

Not just a memory of pain.
No experience in vain.
But an epic Book of You.

Because you chose depth and fire.
Not a wading pool and no flickering flame.
You knew what you were getting into.

one hundred fifty-four

There's a field of wild feminine within me . . .

A rebellious maiden
arriving
in full blossom.

An inner child
exploring with belly
to earth.

A mother
who found the strength
to outgrow her inherited heartache.

A daughter
dreaming herself awake.

one hundred fifty-five

Love, don't rush the light.

Not even the moon

becomes full

in just one night.

one hundred fifty-six

I must be a mermaid,
for the ocean bleeds from my eyes.
Grief and pain are core themes of my lines.
Stories of battle told through
lips that tremble
more than smile.
My hands are soft,
while my edges wild.
I find beauty in strange places.
I get on best with sad, honest faces.
If you try to force me to be happy
or to feel better,
I won't be sorry to disappoint.
So you may as well
stop trying.

one hundred fifty-seven

She laughs.
She growls.
She dances outside the tent.
She's a sip of moonlight
part wolf
and a whole lot of magic.

one hundred fifty-eight

lioness

she can be brave

even while hunting alone

one paw in front of the other

she calms her breath

she believes in herself

more than anyone else

and that's real courage

for she's not led by her mind

but the wild in her heart

her solitude isn't broken

but fearless and graceful

her roar is whole

and she'll leave your body bare

on an altar facing heaven, held by earth

left to become a grassy plain

with only the stars watching

one hundred fifty-nine

Single Mothers:

I have nothing but respect for you. No one can know all that you do until they spend a day in your worn-down shoes. The busyness of the world often neglects your efforts of creating life and raising our future in solitude. You may not have planned it, but you're on a journey for the strong (even on days when you don't feel it). Your arms are full and so is your heart. You're not just something. You're everything to your babies. And you're nothing less than amazing.

one hundred sixty

Waking up during the witching hour to breastfeed my newborn is like being in the wild. Suddenly our apartment has no walls, windows, or doors.

I can sense the trees and smell the earth. The cool breeze that passes relieves me.

We're under the stars, where time and conversation are irrelevant.

We're not planning or preparing, creating art, or doing chores.

The voices aren't screaming in my head. There's no anxiety or stress.

Held by a velvet night and enchanted by a suckling whose heart once drummed in my now hollow womb.

~My Arthur

one hundred sixty-one

I don't want a remedy.
I'm not looking to feel better.
I just need to be under the sky,
in the trees,
my knees skin to dirt,
and my palms
searching Earth's pulse.

one hundred sixty-two

I took a walk today and longed
for the company of another. Not a text.
Not an e-mail. A real voice. Eyes and hands.
The sound of more than just my footsteps.
But no one was there.

I gave in and allowed the air to
taste my tears and the ground
to absorb my yearning.

After a while, I came across a
woman whose face I never saw, but
whose companion gave me everything
I had asked for moments before.

A beautiful female Great Dane turned gently
toward me with big, compassionate eyes that
said it all, "Don't forget me. Don't forget
Mother Earth. I am always here, and I am
always with you. I will hold you when there
are no human arms around. I will listen when
there are no ears to be found. Return to me. I
am here. I am here."

And there she was. And there we were. Not
alone, but together as one.

one hundred sixty-three

Close your eyes.
Open your heart.
Tell your story.
Look around
at who's still there.
Those are your people.

one hundred sixty-four

Your healing
is not a matter of someone else's
time
judgment
or expectation.

You decide when you're over it.
You choose what you want to see.

You determine how your story will end,
continue, and start again.

Like everything else under the sun, you have
time. And your readiness will determine the
beginning of the next season of you.

one hundred sixty-five

I've never meant more to myself than I do
right now. And I've been afraid of dying before
knowing this feeling. I've been through bad, put
myself through worse, and thought that love had
to make me bleed, that it always had to hurt.
But I've grown up a bit. I refuse to go down not
accepting who I am. I've been doing my work
and been down every dark path. I'm stronger
than I've ever been, and I've made good with
my mistakes. Self-love is not what I thought
it to be. It's allowing myself to become new
at any given second, not hiding what I think
others won't like about me. It took a long time
to realize that nobody's love is more important
than my own. To let go of those who don't love
me and release the shame I've been taught.
From here, there's only one way for me to go.
I'm going to love myself the way that sets the
world free. I'm going to love myself the way it
empowers the real me. I've never meant more
to myself than I do right now. And I'll die
knowing this feeling.

one hundred sixty-six

I used to believe
that I had to learn
how to love myself
before I could take care
of myself.

But I've realized that
taking care of myself
is actually teaching me
how to love myself.

one hundred sixty-seven

Truth is,
I've withheld
when I could have given so much.

I've hid among the flock
when I could have led.

I've said nothing
when I had everything to say.

I've pretended to be one hundred other people
because I thought no one wanted who I was.

And I've chosen fear and anger
over company and poetry.

Now I realize: That's no longer me
and there's no more time
for pretending.

one hundred sixty-eight

Thank you, patterns of my life,
for all the times
you've woken me up,
shown me what's wrong,
and incessantly asked me,

"Now, what are you going to do about it?"

one hundred sixty-nine

I'm holding space for you, sister. I'm not the kind of woman to look away when you talk about rape, abuse, or addiction. I won't flinch when you walk in covered in dirt. I won't judge your story of neglect, betrayal, or trauma. I won't try to rewrite your suicidal thoughts or self-hatred. I won't ignore your cry. I won't back away from your drool, vomit, or blood. I won't deny the relationship you have with your womb, work, or the unseen. I won't belittle how you see yourself. I won't pretend to have an answer for you. I won't compare your divorce, breakup, or loss to another. I believe you. I believe what you say you've been through, what you're going through, and what you're carrying with you. I believe it when you say that you've tried and that you will pull through. I believe you now, and I will continue believing in you. Because I am the kind of woman who holds space. For you, sister.

one hundred seventy

Your truth will bring out the worst in others.
Your love will tingle what they've numbed.
Your authenticity will provoke
closed minds.
Your gratitude will irritate trolls.
Your success will attract haters.
Your empowerment will create enemies.
Your uniqueness will antagonize fear.
Your courage will attract cowards.
Your sexuality will freak people out.
Your joy will tug at their trauma.
Your compassion will unmask envy.
And love, that's what it's meant to do.
Your aliveness will reveal many mental prisons,
but help to set even more minds free.

one hundred seventy-one

Sometimes I'd rather
be misunderstood
than have to justify
my pain.

one hundred seventy-two

Blessed Are Those Who Disappoint

Who show up in pieces, but refuse to fall apart.
Who carry what no one wants to acknowledge,
but are dying to see. Who have nothing to offer,
but something real to say. Whose loss has made
them whole. Who are discovering an irrefutable
authenticity. Whose scary story made them
brave enough to tell it. Who have been pushed
behind a hard wall, but whose hearts remain
soft. Whose souls won't leave them alone. Who
live outside the box with no plan to get in.
Who can't wipe the battle from their peaceful
eyes. Who get knocked down but get up again,
and again, and again. Who can't forget, but
help us remember that the transformation of
our pain from burden to soulful purpose can
translate into not fitting in. Who are thankful
to have failed conformity and grateful to
disappoint if it means holding space to heal, to
do better, to wake up. Amen.

one hundred seventy-three

When your self-worth dims
and the colors fade, seek the
stories of those who created
great change.

one hundred seventy-four

The first time I heard
Lionel Richie sing,
my six-year-old self cried. The
hole in my chest was seen.
Was she looking for me?
I didn't know where my
mother was. And I had no clue
what to do. But knowing
that Lionel was out there
singing my blues made
me feel less alone because
maybe he missed his mom
too.

one hundred seventy-five

Oh, girl.
How you ache.
How you break.
The way you go.
The way you stay.
How you bleed.
How you breathe.
The way you love.
The way you hate.
How you give.
How you take.
The way you lure.
The way you cure.
How you ache.
How you break.
Girl, I love you.

one hundred seventy-six

When in darkness,
the passing of time
can feel like agony.

Anger can last
an afternoon. Grief
can take a summer.

But there's nothing
more empowering
than a woman who can
pace herself while
on the path of
shadow.

Who knows that dark
times aren't about
beating the clock,
but a being season of
resilience.

one hundred seventy-seven

The night I met
the big bad wolf
he walked away a king.
I left a wounded sheep
who for decades
forgot she was a queen.

one hundred seventy-eight

Even when
a part of you is
painfully dying,
despite feeling
as if you've lost yourself,
you barely recognize life,
and it's hard to breathe,
she reminds you
that where you are
right now
is where all the power is at.

one hundred seventy-nine

Yesterday, the ocean of my heart ran over.
I cried at least one hundred times. I grieved
many things—the woman who dreamt of
a natural childbirth, the desperate teenager
who prayed for love or death, the inner child
who craved her mother and longed to feel
the arms of family around her. I cried for
my gentle grandfather who died when I was
barely ten and for my fierce grandmother
who followed as I turned fourteen. I cried
for my Native American ancestry. I cried
for my father who used to say, "Take it like
a man, or take it like a mouse," before he'd
spank me. I cried for all the hungry children
in the world. I cried for those we hide and
shun. I cried for those stuck in war. I cried
for Earth. I cried for the fading forests. I
cried for those who've experienced death,
loss, disease, addiction, abuse, depression,
abandonment, and neglect. I cried for the
injustices done to women and children.
I cried for the men who aren't given a
chance. I cried for those who are wrongly
imprisoned. I cried for all the mistreated
animals of the world and for those living
and dying in factory farms. I cried for the
hungry polar bear, the starving wolves, and
the disappearing buffalo. I cried and cried

because yesterday the ocean of my heart
ran over.

~January 3, 2019

one hundred eighty

I love the ones
who are two parts crazy
and a portrait of poetry.
I love the ones
with an intention
covered in wild dreams.
I love the ones
who don't always roar
but the quiet ones
who feel deeply,
are awkward at goodbyes,
and have secret talents
like walking through fire.

one hundred eighty-one

Don't write to be liked.
Don't write to be right.
Don't write to be understood.

Write to become
emotionally literate,
accepting of yourself,
and free.

Write to move a culture.
Write a philosophical change.
Write to revolutionize your pain.

one hundred eighty-two

Give yourself
the best possible chance
to discover who you are
when the pain is gone.

one hundred eighty-three

We're unconventional.
We're untraditional.
We're awkward.
We're grace.
We're every age, color, size, and shape.
We're unfamiliar.
We're known.
We're taboo.
We're outcasts, wallflowers, dreamers, and
leaders.
We're howling at the moon.
We're highly sensitive.
We're intuitive.
We're creators and creative.
We're weird.
We're the change stagnancy feared.
We're mothers, sisters, and daughters.
We're a revolutionary vision.
We're warriors.
We're women.

one hundred eighty-four

I asked the ocean
to tell me about myself.
And it said,
Come in. Deeper.
Deeper, child!
There's no glory
without guts.
There's no blessing
without bravery.
And when you walk back
out of here, you'll know
it was never about
letting go, holding on,
or control, but letting
the floor drop out
from beneath you and
being held by
your soul.

one hundred eighty-five

Not everyone will be there for you. Not everyone will understand your tears, your pain, or your fears. Not everyone will be able to witness your vulnerability or stay when you lose your shit. Not everyone can handle your mess or what's causing you stress. Not everyone will believe how much it hurts or want to hear it. But those who have bled, loved, and lost will. They'll circle around like warm bees to a queen. They'll pray at your side through your tribulations. They won't turn away from your suffering or treat it like it's contagious. Because they know what you'll soon find out, that there's beauty in a breakdown, that there's awe before and after a storm, that what doesn't kill you will make you stronger.

one hundred eighty-six

There's a changing of the guards happening right now inside of you. Peace has found her way. Grace and her cavalry are here to stay. There are archangels on your side. Waiting for your sign. You can no longer deny it. If you don't believe me, ask your soul. And it will whisper: "Surrender, and let my love swallow you whole."

one hundred eighty-seven

She's the kind of water
that finds her way to heaven
makes rainbows
and like a waterfall
gushes a mama
kind of love.

one hundred eighty-eight

I sip sweet tea
with my fear.
And pick flowers
with my anger.
I soak my sadness
in sunlight
and my hopelessness
in salt water.
I let myself
be a home
to all of me.

~Self-Therapy

one hundred eighty-nine

To Albert Leo and Arthur Holger,

For all the ways I didn't show up for you.
For all the times I couldn't comfort you.
For any moment you felt unloved.
It was never because of you.
It was because of me.

Love,
Mama

one hundred ninety

When you've prayed to every angel. When you've chanted all the names of every goddess. When the sage is gone. When the candles have burned out. When hope and prayer respond, "You're it." When the only way through is taking on the mountain. When you loosen the death grip on control. When grace is dozing off on your chest. When nocturnal instincts awaken your heart. When, for the first time in your life, you want to breathe deeply and feel your muscles. When you hear your ancestors telling stories in your bones. When you realize pain is all the colors of a sunset and is sometimes only visible through a collective lens. When you quit anointing yourself with the past. When you stop covering your scent. When sadness no longer feels like anesthesia. When love tastes like coffee. When your soul says, "We'll be better at the end of this." When you believe it's true. When you give this newness a chance and wake up to find you're already halfway up the summit.

one hundred ninety-one

Learning to allow
any unpleasant reaction
to your story of pain
lights a brave flame
that will bring more light,
warmth, and attention
needed to the issue—for you
and anyone else
already sitting
around that fire.

one hundred ninety-two

Emotional pain is an untapped sustainable
resource of
possibility
imagination
creativity
beauty
art
empowerment
leadership
and change.

one hundred ninety-three

Love, don't you know yet
that your heart is like the sun
that burns away my pain?
Your embrace is like the moon
that soothes my aches.
Love, don't you know yet
that your light
creates a path
day and night
from my heart to yours?

~For Christian

one hundred ninety-four

I sometimes
wonder about your eyes.
And how good
they are at seeing.
Because when you
look at me,
I feel like the person
I've always dreamt
of being.

one hundred ninety-five

Let it be disruptive. Let it be a movement. Let it be about connection. Let it feel new. Let it be a return. Let it spread. Let it be different. Let it feed peace. Let it be about personal growth. Let it be a revolutionary expression. Let it be empowering. Let it bring people together. Let it be crazy. Let it kick your ass. Let it be cool. Let it be love. Let it be a weird dose of something real. Let it come alive. Let it bring you to life. Let it be a beautiful message. Let it be big. Let it take time. Let it be relevant. Let it be about freedom. Let it be about looking in. Let it be about seeing each other. Let it be about you.

one hundred ninety-six

While the moon dozed
upon the world, she sunk
deep into blankets
of isolation. Another
day followed by an infinite
collection of bad words
drooled from her mouth
until unconsciousness
carried her into darkness
dotted with a
few dangling stars.

one hundred ninety-seven

Love, do you remember that
day I called you in tears and asked
to take a drive?

We silently held hands until
I remembered how to breathe.

Our souls know each other. Not
a word needs to be spoken.
That is us.

Love, that day, I never told you,
but you healed me with your
quiet tenderness.

And one day, if you need it,
I'll be there to pick you up too.

one hundred ninety-eight

I went to see a plastic surgeon about
the state of my nose and my too-thin lips.
In the waiting room, there weren't before and
after pics of models, but burn victims and child
survivors of horrific accidents. I felt disgusting
to be so superficial, but I couldn't get up and
leave.

The doctor was cold and unfriendly. His fingers
prodded my face with judgment. But when he
finished with the examination, he said to my
twenty-three-year-old soul:

You don't need to change anything.
You have to consider the whole.
See the big picture of you.

I was reborn in that sterile examination room.
And from that day forward, I stopped seeking
any procedure that would change me into the
woman I wasn't born to be.

one hundred ninety-nine

If you find yourself having to tiptoe around others, you aren't walking among your tribe.

two hundred

Blessed be the measurement
of your heart's deepest longing.

The pain
the fear
and all the shattered glass
blessed be the fire
that turns it all to ash.

Your massacred roots
drowned in moonlight,
blessed be the water
that midwives your fairy insight.

The hysteria
lunacy
and grieving.

The talons
the wheat seed
your dragon's heavy breathing.

Your rising
and resurrection
sacred potion
of inner medicine.

Your artistic braids
the heroine's journey
the shadow you're naming
with no need to hurry.

The descent
the quest
the glimpse of mystical glory.

The shape-shifting.
The dancing.
You are every character of this epic story.

Your tendrils
are carried
by a messenger called Air.

The earth is
nourished
by your morning prayer.

Twice born and unswaddled,
together we'll stand.

She'll always be next to you,
sword in hand.

And with Her vast wingspan,

high above,
you'll hear them whisper:

I see you.
I hear you.
You are nothing but love.

Blessed be the measurement
of your heart's deepest longing.

Your bloodstained stone
your wild chalice
and high altar.

Blessed be, sister,
this path you cannot falter.

two hundred one

Someone once said to me,
"Don't forget where you come from."
As if I could.
Leaving that broken home
is what made me whole.

two hundred two

You're more than the sum total
of your pain.

You've got the formula
to heal.

You are an equation
of love.

two hundred three

The oak knows where I am
and it knows the way home.

The roots of the Nordic birch
remind me that I, too, am rooted
in both the seen and the hidden.

The beech shows me how to take the rain
and shine of night and day. (The ravens know
their other names.)

The yew speaks to me in feathers
and during the darkest moments before dawn.

While visions of the gold willow dance in my
heart even when the stars are gone.

The trees know what to do.
And they'll tell us if we ask them.

~Ode to Trees

two hundred four

Because, love,
when you make it hard for others to get in,
you make it hard for you too.

two hundred five

Sometimes you don't
know your purpose
until you sit
in a circle
with fearless people.

two hundred six

She turns you toward freedom every single
time. Despite fear. No matter the pain. And
she does it with love. She pulls you from the
wreckage and calls you out. She sets fire to the
cage of doubt around your power. She speaks
the language of your scars. And mid-battle,
she offers you reflection. Your own. You see
yourself in the eyes of your warrior sister
and know that tonight there will be no sweet
surrender.

two hundred seven

You can't hide from your inner shit. Nope.
You can't sleep it off. You can't surgically
remove it. You can't eat, buy, wish, or exercise
it away. You have to turn toward it and
embrace it. Look into its eyes; be patient and
so tender. Then get intimate with it until it
shows you another way and a different you.

two hundred eight

Be present
in the state
you're in.

Your heart,
a nation
of love.

Your soul,
a continent
of possibility.

two hundred nine

Blessed Are the Rejected

To those who've been refused attention,
acknowledgment, or love, it's time to whisper
a final sweet goodbye. And every time that
cord grows back, cut it off. You've changed.
They haven't. Your heart is open. Theirs isn't.
Your river needs to flow, and it's time to open
the dam. Blood doesn't always mean family.
"No" doesn't translate into "never." Hold on to
yourself, pray with reckless abandon to be free,
and don't return to paths that don't serve you.

two hundred ten

Sometimes science isn't the answer.
Sometimes intuition is.

Sometimes structure isn't the answer.
Sometimes the abstract is.

Sometimes debate isn't the answer.
Sometimes holding space is.

Sometimes doubt isn't the answer.
Sometimes faith is.

Sometimes balance isn't the answer.
Sometimes going all in is.

Sometimes happiness isn't the answer.
Sometimes empowerment is.

Sometimes silence isn't the answer.
Sometimes expression is.

Sometimes conformity isn't the answer.
Sometimes authenticity is.

Sometimes being sorry isn't the answer.
Sometimes being relentless is.

two hundred eleven

When women gather in circle and share
stories, a fire is lit. And the scorched space
within that circle becomes fertile soil for
possibility, imagination, and compassion.
When women connect through their stories,
Earth listens, dreams, and takes them into her
womb and asks, "Can you feel the embryonic
kicks of a new world?" And more often than
not, these women leave reborn from stories
of pain.

two hundred twelve

If you've had a hard time
replacing pain with love,
you're not alone.

Embrace all of you.

It takes more than
the sun to make
a rainbow.

two hundred thirteen

I've grown
from blaming everyone else
to taking responsibility for my story
from looking outside for the missing parts
to finding the answers within myself
from playing the fragile voiceless girl
to becoming a strong, roaring woman
from having a fear-based mentality
to living with a courageous, abundant heart
from feeling embarrassed
for the space I take up
to holding my own with pride
from being unable to fight my own battles
to an army of one.

two hundred fourteen

Tonight I light a candle
for all the seasons and shades of loneliness—for
all the lonely souls wishing for more warmth
and company—for the brave ones calling in
community, intimacy,
and conversation.
This flame is for you.
Burn brightly.
So we know
where to find you.

two hundred fifteen

When our story of pain
becomes a river
wild and free
a source that carries
moonlight to the sea.

When our story of pain
becomes the sky
wide and noticed
a place heaven nests
open like a lotus.

When our story of pain
becomes the earth
strong and nourished
where love is human
a path of courage.

two hundred sixteen

Every story told weaves a cloak
that is passed around
to ready shoulders
like a meadow returned
to the crow and bee
like a crown returned
to an exiled queen.

two hundred seventeen

When a gentle hand
brushes tears from your face
not to stop your crying
but to help the salt and water
do their work
and wash the pain away.

two hundred eighteen

I told my bestie that I felt broken.
She said I was hilarious.
I almost smiled.

And then she said,

Even though you feel broken, you sound so spirited still. I love that you have so much soul even though it may not feel like it. Girl, I can still feel your awesome energy. I love you.

And that's what I needed to hear.

two hundred nineteen

Acceptance
is the ultimate forgiveness
because it gives
you the freedom
to move on
and live your life
as you choose to.

two hundred twenty

Busyness won't hold you accountable.

A program can't make you feel enough.

Overcompensation will never change the parts you hate.

Self-imposed repression isn't anti-inflammatory.

Pretending will never soothe emotional wounds.

Hiding and numbing doesn't work.

Staying in the victim role doesn't change that you are the hero of your own life.

two hundred twenty-one

Self-love
is a home
within me
that allows
every emotion
to express, exist,
to come and go
like four
walls,
a high ceiling,
and wooden floors,
rooms, windows,
a table, and door.
Feelings come and go
but love never leaves.

two hundred twenty-two

My pelvic floor
isn't a revolving door
it's a path to my womb
a sacred room
that connects me to earth
a space where I give birth
to babies, ecstasy, and creativity.

two hundred twenty-three

You can choose love.
No matter the
circumstances.
You can have the
worst night,
choose love,
and wake up
with a belly
full of hopeful stars.

two hundred twenty-four

The language of love that my mother spoke
was always through shame, regret, and fear—
for not being there and for not being able to
make different choices.

(Why we don't understand each other.)

two hundred twenty-five

Stay and I will hold your secrets
and all of your mistakes.
I will hold your failures
and all of your aches. Stay.
Let me hold this pain for you.
Even for just a moment or two.
Because soon, I may need
you to hold mine too.

two hundred twenty-six

Catch yourself.
When you care for someone.
Catch yourself.
When you know their story.
Catch yourself.
When you know you can't be present.
Catch yourself.
When they start to share what's hurting their heart.
Catch yourself.
So you don't respond impatiently, judge unintentionally, or use their wounds against them.
Catch yourself.
So you don't project, assign shame, or unintentionally add a layer of blame.
Catch yourself.
And use this as a moment to practice a two-way kind of love.
Catch yourself.
And hold sacred space.

two hundred twenty-seven

I was thinking about all the people I hold
captive in my heart because of
betrayal
abandonment
and rejection
and it started to get hard to breathe.
My heart became overburdened with
hardness that needed to be set free.

~Your Heart Is No Prison

two hundred twenty-eight

She'll never know
the full glory
of the sky
using someone
else's wings
to fly.

two hundred twenty-nine

The thing about her is
even when she doesn't know
what to say
she stays.

two hundred thirty

We're under the same sky. But the air isn't the same. My feet touch the earth. But I don't recognize these names. I walk these streets. But feel invisible. A push for recognition. A fight of perception. A new consideration. The opposite of segregation.

I'm humbled. I'm humbled! I'm down on my knees. The hardest part, will you trust me? The hardest part, will you give me a chance? The hardest part, will you see . . .

These hands. My heart. These eyes. My mind. I've learned the language of this land. Yet can't be included. Am I just a label? Am I just a woman? (Am I not just, a human?)

Respect. Equality. Diversity. Inclusion. I want connection. Community! I want a revolution!

Mothers. Servers. Doctors. Teachers. Nurses. Artists. Poets. Leaders. I'm no longer a foreigner in a foreign land. I'm not just an ethnicity. I want to give a hand. Socially. Economically. Culturally. Doesn't it all come down to humanity?

Communication. Integration. A common foundation. I'm a mother, daughter, neighbor, a part of this nation.

Like you, I have bills to pay. Like you, I have dreams to pursue. I will grow old in this country, but before I do, I want to go farther with you.

We know where we're going. Solidarity. Unity. An empowered femininity. So what will my story be? Will it be limiting or liberating?

Will someone remember that I existed if these old norms aren't challenged and tested?

I'm no longer standing alone or trying to make my skin thicker. Can we write a new set of rules and give the world a new way to live?

I am a woman in this country. I have a gift to give. I am a woman in this country. I have a gift to give. The hardest part. Will you see me? The hardest part. Will you sit with me and dream?

~Immigrant Women

two hundred thirty-one

Sister,
I'll be your lungs
when you cannot breathe.
I'll be your arms.
when you can't receive.
I'll hold space
when it's hard to just be.
I'll be your wings
when you don't feel free.

two hundred thirty-two

When I catch myself seeking validation, waiting for approval, or asking permission to express my authentic self, I throw up a little in my mouth. Then I summon my dragon to burn that old inner house to the ground.

two hundred thirty-three

When you stop trying
to fit into a world
that you don't belong to anymore,
you grow
and automatically start a new one
but with relaxed shoulders,
more laughter,
and way more magic.

two hundred thirty-four

Remind your inner child:
It wasn't that you were unlovable.
It was that they were incapable of love.

two hundred thirty-five

As I wept
in the arms of darkness,
I heard the voice of my grandmother say,
Nothing stays the same, darling,
not even pain.
Life is a path of change.
Of ecstasy and ache.
So, no matter what the storm claims,
let love light the way.

two hundred thirty-six

I've been through
many cycles of pain
only to be reborn again
and again,
each time
different, new,
and more comfortable
in my skin.

two hundred thirty-seven

To the woman on fire:

I won't tell you
that you're radiant right now.

I won't tell you
how you light up the dark.

I won't tell you
that you make me a believer.

I won't tell you
how your change inspires.

I won't tell you
how one day your courage
will birth a new, stronger forest.

two hundred thirty-eight

To the unexpected,
to death and loss,
to sickness and injury,
to the loneliness that walks
hand in hand with change,
to pain and suffering, fear,
rejection, heartbreak, and betrayal,
to the hardest year of your life,
to darkness—
to all of it making you stronger, truer, freer,
more beautiful, and whole.

two hundred thirty-nine

Darkness may feel hard,
but it's the only way to show
how love makes it
all look so easy.

two hundred forty

Letting go sucks. It's sad. It's confusing. It's lonely and messed up. It hits you like a raging freight train and burns through your chest like a lightning bolt. It makes you crave a real good numbing. You pray to freeze time. You just want to sleep. You beg it to quit. But it won't. No mercy, baby. Retch. You dry heave from your soul and realize this threat to your entire existence is quite beautiful. It's grace, and it's breathtaking aliveness. Exhale now. Look at you there. Radiant, on your own two feet, all anchored to Earth. You have the strength of an archangel. Now, cut the cord. Let go. Let go and gaze into your future and see that goddamn radiant rainbow.

two hundred forty-one

Your story of pain
deserves a resting place
in the Book of You.
Place it all there—
you can always go back
to those pages to show
how much you've grown
between then and now.

two hundred forty-two

If I ever have a little girl,
I will teach her what it means to be naïve
that monsters are real
and that she doesn't have to please
anyone or anything
especially those who take "no" for "yes"
or even maybe
that she is a queen
and that self-love will never require her
to bow down
or need a king.

two hundred forty-three

Sometimes the world's sages come from abusive
homes,
our gurus from poverty,
our teachers from AA,
our poets from prison,
our prophets from the projects.

Sometimes our saints don't wake up privileged
with the vision of a better future, but with the
challenge of surviving the day.

Because God works in mysterious ways.

Sometimes freedom comes from betrayal,
courage from regret,
hope from loss,
love from disbelief,
vitality from horror,
motivation from rage,
and beauty from suffering.

Sometimes what's right comes from that which
is wrong, unexpectedly bringing light to dark
days.

Because God works in mysterious ways.

two hundred forty-four

Earth and Air.
Fire and Ice.
Mother of Dark.
Father of Light.
A newborn spark.
On the darkest night.

~Winter Solstice

two hundred forty-five

Let the story of who you were
send shivers down the spines
of our granddaughters.
Let them hear about you
as the woman who was "herself"
who did her own thing
and helped others along the way.

two hundred forty-six

You're the black sheep
born with the resilience
of Nature.
You, little lamb,
were gifted with the pain to bring change.
You, seemingly fragile flower,
can forget about your blood
and remember
you have
heaven for a sister,
a forest for an aunt,
and the ocean for a mother.
Now stop forgetting your power.

two hundred forty-seven

This autumn
strip down to your soul.
Let go.
Let go.
Go naked
to the funeral of your old self.
Let go.
Let go.
Bare your soul this season.
Even the trees go naked into the dark.

two hundred forty-eight

Only consider
the opinions of those
who are sitting with you around the fire
who aren't afraid of the burn of change
or the sweat of possibility
of what it means
to nurture the flames
of your own heart
and make this place better.

two hundred forty-nine

Healing is fucking messy. It's alienation. It's detachment. It's batshit crazy. It's jet-black inky darkness. It makes you ache for the void or the mundane. You want to quit everything, but you can't. You won't. Not now. Not ever, baby. Because even though it aches the mother of all aches, you've changed. Underneath all the bullshit, there you are. Brand new. Born again. An angel awakened to her cosmic mission. And you aren't going back. There are more out there, waking up in the dark. So don't worry about fixing any part of you and let your wicked shambles raise the damn roof on this whole thing.

two hundred fifty

Forgiving

For giving

Betrayal, thank you
for giving me clarity.

Heartbreak, thank you
for giving me freedom.

Suffering, thank you
for giving me wisdom.

Failure, thank you
for giving me another chance.

two hundred fifty-one

And the day was good enough
and she was crazy enough
to believe that everything
was going to be okay
enough to feel
all that wasn't rational
that made the least sense
enough to reveal
the unknown within her
and that was enough
to make her say:

I'm not afraid anymore.

two hundred fifty-two

I free myself from the past.
I let go of habits and routines
that hold me back.
I release the toxins in my body.
I break poisonous soul contracts
with friends and family.
I express my creativity.
I make healthy boundaries.
I'm open to new realms of healing.
I forgive myself.
I call my power home.

two hundred fifty-three

I want to be that for you.
That friend.
That sign.
That call.
That hand that lifts you back to the surface.
To remind you that you don't have to carry any
burden alone, that there's nothing to be
ashamed of, and that there is a world out there
that wants you to be a part of it.
That needs you and loves you.
That believes in you.

You are not alone.

two hundred fifty-four

It took me a lifetime of years,
and getting over myself,
and trusting,
and believing
to give in to the wisdom
that if I want
to be loved,
I must be love.
That if I want
to be beautiful,
I must choose
to nourish myself
and others
beautifully.
That if I want
to be free,
I must forgive.
Because I don't deserve
to remain on any hook
when my wings
belong to the sky.

two hundred fifty-five

Remember who you were when you pulled through the darkest night of the soul.

Remember how you rallied, how you remained functional, even if barely.

Remember how you changed, defied your genetics, and kept going.

Remember how you held it together as everything else fell apart.

Remember all the times you were stronger than you felt and wiser than you thought.

Remember how you had a galaxy within you when you thought yourself empty.

Remember, so the next time when you know you're going to need a wildfire instead of a match to get through the darkness remember the survivor within.

flower
signs

each sign corresponds with your month of birth

You are
a thousand
graceful movements
and
a galaxy
filled with a trillion stars.

You are
the ecstatic
sum
of sunshine
darkness
and flowers.

january

Carnation Woman

She reminds you that it isn't power or energy that you need to survive this season, but wisdom—and that you will receive it if you are courageous enough to bare your soul while traveling through the valley of winter. She brings life to dark times and unveils resilience and endurance. She's the faithful light that speckles the path of shadow and the fierce flower that blossoms in the midst of death and decay. She's the awe and wonder of all that is untouched and tranquil. She's the howling of the wind and wolves and a protective quilt of snow. And she isn't a slow, painful death but the third trimester giving birth to a stronger, truer version of you.

february

Violet Woman

She's a dream weaver. She's heart-shaped,
humble, and will help you remember how
to navigate high winds, strong tides, and the
season of transition. She feels like the spark
of something new and can ignite a flame of
hope. She's the waking dream. She's growth
and stillness. Where there was once death, she
blossoms. She's the vibration of truth, self-
worth, and sympathy. She's the kind of
innocence that takes fearless responsibility.
She's the last bend through the valley of
winter and the light at the end of the tunnel.
She is the eternal symbol of love.

march

Daffodil Woman

She's the waking dawn of spring, the light of abundance, a silver lining, and the warmth of the returning sun. She marks the path leading out of the underworld. She's the last hours of the great slumber. She's a new beginning. And she'll take you to spiritual places and help you to navigate new lovers, friendships, and love.

april

Daisy Woman

She'll remind you to play, to put flowers in your hair, and press your belly to earth. She's innocent, pure, and simple. A little sun, even while it rains, and a specimen of beauty— she's festive and walks the path of the light each day. She's cheerful and a true blessing. She's usually early and lasts the length of a hot summer. She is a breath of fresh air. She brings a sense of community to those who feel alone, and safety to those threatened. She's a relief for overwhelming emotions and allows you the realization and confidence that everything is going to be okay night or day.

may

Lily of the Valley Woman

She banishes winter and renews life. She's
the carrier of hope and the sender of joy.
She is the return of happiness. She's a full
belly, protective mother, and the fragrance
of enchanting nectar. She attracts magic and
rings when the unseen sings. She'll help you to
remember what has been long forgotten: that
a new world is rising and it is heaven on earth.

june

Rose Woman

She's the full sunbathing beauty. She's medicinal, noble, and fragrant. She doesn't thrive in crowded places, but blossoms on her own. She's social but doesn't try to prove herself. She's the crown and the confetti. She's the luscious symbol of love and a sensual invitation. She's the crone, maidenhood, and the goddess. She's grounded, empathetic, powerful, and healing. And her love, loyalty, and virtue are stronger than any thorn. She is the queen of summer solstice.

july

Larkspur Woman

She's a long summer day and a symbol of success. She'll remind you of your talents and have you believing in what you can become. She dispels negativity and is a colorful life enthusiast. She strengthens bonds, celebrates uniqueness, and will get your attention without even trying.

august

Poppy Woman

She is the life after a living death. She's the energy of the moon and has invisibility superpowers. She's an eternal night's rest and a sacred source of protection. She has a lively imagination and delivers her messages in dreams. She offers consolation, extravagance, and intensity. And she'll help you to cultivate a richer, more peaceful, and beautiful life.

september

Aster Woman

She's luscious and wild. She's a talisman of love and a symbol of patience. She's charming, patient, and wards off the cold-blooded. She sends high vibrations and conveys contentment. She welcomes autumn and reveals the beauty of the season. Some say she's fallen stardust that's blossomed on Earth's surface. She makes honey taste sweeter and is the best symbol of affection.

october

Marigold Woman

She's carried by the rain and is the return of spirit. She marks the descent into the dark season. She's the pregnant belly of autumn and dresses in the colors of dying leaves. She's versatile and bright, a last herb of sunshine. She'll remind you of your passion, creativity, and strength. She begins the descent toward the valley of winter.

november

Chrysanthemum Woman

She'll line the procession to your old self's funeral. She's a celebration for all that you were and everything you'll become. She's the seed of optimism and longevity. She blesses the living with radiance, energy, and abundance. She'll summon your bravery and your sense of humor. She'll walk you hand in hand, strong and proud, to the gates of the underworld and will leave you there dancing and sweating. She is the reminder of your ability to grow in every facet of your life, but especially in the coming season.

december

Narcissus Woman

She brings faith and teachings of respect.
She's calming and anoints tough and
unknown times with peace. She is the flower
of the underworld. She reminds us that
although we may feel hopeless and fragile, a
victim to the season of our emotions, those
dark spaces are also a source of beauty and
strength. She holds the wisdom of the last
cycle of every life, the remaining sliver that
makes us whole and new again and again.

stay close

Bookmark:
theshebook.com

Instagram:
@thugunicorn @tanyamarkul

did any of these words touch you?

I'd love to hear from you.

Write to me:
tanya@theshebook.com

about the author

Tanya Markul started writing when she was six years old. She used to scribble lines on top of lines and called it "poetry." Early in life, she discovered emotional pain to be a sustainable resource for her work—and she hasn't stopped writing since. Her themes explore heartache, loss, abandonment, rejection, and mental health. In her words, she writes for the "rejected ones" and to "revolutionize pain." Her quotes, stories, poems, and prose have touched readers around the world. She hopes to be a source of inspiration and empowerment for years to come.

Believe
in
what
you
can
become.

Thank you, Dearest Reader.
Thank you with all of my heart.

Unapologetically illuminate
at what
you can control.
The sun
doesn't stop shining
because someone feels
it's too bright.